SEATTLE GRAFFITI

An off-The-Wall
Collection Stolen By
BoB Sheffels

GOOSES BY
PETE SMITH

Sheffelsonian Press

122 17th Ave. E.
Seattle, WA 98112

Extreme thanks to Jennifer Solid, for her help and for her existence in my life.

Magnified thanks to Ben Dennis, samaritan and coach; Peter Smith, talented artist; and graffiti hunter Aileen Fink.

Thanks to Carol Brown, Greg Singleton, Paul Kotz, Beth Jones, Connie Kenyon and a few others.

Contents

I gave them their chance.

Before this book went on the stands I took it to certain high-ranking officals of the Seattle Chamber of Commerce and plunked it down on their conference table. "Ten thousand dollars and it's yours," I told them. "Nobody but us has to know the truth about Seattle. Nobody but us has to know that beneath this exterior of pleasant green hills overlooking sparkling blue waters are incredibly ugly scabs; that behind the scrubbed faces and friendly smiles of Seattle's citizens are disgustingly sick minds. Nobody but us has to know that this city is a teeming slimebucket of assorted degenerates who probably don't even change their socks every day."

I exited, leaving behind the bathroom expose that would surely drop Seattle from the ranks of America's ten most livable cities down into the FBI's listing of "entire cities that should be deported to Paraguay." I closed the door behind me.

Four days later I received a postcard of the Space Needle. On the back it said that the Seattle landmark was erected in 1962 and then there was this message:

Dear Blackmailer:

Quite an erection, eh? You are cordially invited to sit on it and then take a flying leap.

Yours truly,
The Seattle Chamber of Commerce

So there you have it, the whole sordid story behind this revealing book. It is with reluctance that I present it to you at the public service price of only $4.95. I much would have preferred a $10,000 payoff.

Now that you know me as naught but a mercenary cad, allow this note of compassion.

Realize as you thumb through these pages that most of this graffiti comes from bathrooms, those intimate cubicles that serve as substitute confessionals for those of us who are not Catholic. It is necessary for all of us to expel things from our minds, just was we expel wastes rotting inside our bodies before they make us sick. Efficiency requires that all this expelling be done at the same time and in the same place—the bathroom. If you find this graffiti of Seattle to be twisted, crude, cynical and funny only in the most common sort of way, remember also that it is healthy for its authors.

One final comment before we go on to the graffiti. You can not pull graffiti from the fertile, sweaty wall of a bathroom, run it through a typewriter, and transplant it onto a virginal white page without losing a little vitality. The following steps are recommended for counteracting this regrettable loss.

1. Have a beer or a frozen daiquiri or a 24-ounce shot of whiskey or something.

2. Your pants are too tight. Unbutton the top button.

3. Hell, while you're at it, you might as well go sit down and take a load off your kidneys.

4. Take the book with you.

5. Ahhhhhhhh!

On to the graffiti.

Blast!

Sorry about the delay, but something has come up. These damn geese got into the graffiti and I can't get them out.

It happened at Green Lake. I was lying in the grass over by Duck Island, working on the manuscript, when there was this wreck. A fat man on roller skates went wide on a curve and flattened a puppy and a housewife pushing two baby carriages. Horrible thing. I ran over to gawk, of course, and while I was gone these two geese got into the graffiti. I don't know how, they just did. Okay?

They appear to be a couple—geese mate for life— and they are quite territorial. They hissed at me when I tried to chase them out and turned down a bribe of an eight-month's supply of Wonderbread, so there's nothing I can do.

We're stuck with them, folks. We're just going to have to make the best of a bad situation here and pretend it's normal to have geese running loose in the graffiti.

You won't hear me say another goddamn word about them.

On to the graffiti.

WOMEN ON MEN & SEX & THINGS

Throughout history, women have been born without penises.

As this trend continues, more and more women are growing to resent the biological fact that they can't have a penis without having a man. The problem here is that men are very attached to their penises (and vice versa) and expect gratitude and servitude from any woman they consent to share this wonder stud with.

Women who are now grandmothers coped with this unreasonable male expectation by pretending to play along, and almost always managed to tame the penises they worked with. Now, younger, more impetuous women want the rules changed so that they get extra points for stealing the penis outright and claiming it as a trophy. Men have balked at this proposed amendment and the result is a lot of grabbing and pulling that causes friction and hard, uh...feelings.

Being more demonstrative than their male counterparts, and more likely to need an emotional safety valve, women write bad things about men sometimes on bathroom walls and feel all better.

If upon your pee I sit
you're an inconsiderate shit
Rio Cafe (women's)

A lucky woman has always
made love, never been fucked
Comet Tavern (women's)

Faster, Baby, Faster
Virginia Inn (women's)

Double your pleasure
Double your fun
Xerox your clit
O'Banion's Tavern (women's)

A climax a day
keeps the doctor away
The Duchess Tavern (women's)

Some like them thick
some like them thin
I'll take anything
that fits in
Rio Cafe (women's)

If you don't want a good time,
call Robert 328-_____
... and then

For premature ejaculation
call Robert 328-_____
... and then

Tell him to try the
squeeze method
by Masters & Johnson
UW parking garage

Michael _____ doesn't
need a woman, he needs a
mirror with a hole in it
Comet Tavern (women's)

Sex and rain are alike in
Seattle. You never know
how long it will last or
how many inches you'll get.
O'Banion's Tavern (women's)

Men have the plumbing
but, oh,
we women have the features
Watertown (women's)

I went out with him for a year,
never lied or let him down—
and he dumps me!
Art Building UofW (women's)

Better to have loved and lost
than to have spent your whole
damn life with him.

The Duchess Tavern (women's)

As of 08/24/82
I hate love

Comet Tavern (women's)

A good man is hard to find

... and then

A hard man is good to find

... and then

A hard man is good to eat

Comet Tavern (women's)

I like to eat um raw!

Rainbow Tavern (women's)

What's the best thing a woman
can get out of a penis?
The wrinkles.

Rainbow Tavern

If you meet a man
without a smile
give him yours

Buckaroo Tavern (women's)

Define "Man"
1. Never knows what he wants
   but tells you anyway
2. Sex-crazed maniac

Music Building UofW (sound room)

The more I know men
The better I like my dog

The Duchess Tavern (women's)

What's the difference
between like & love?
Spit and swallow

Blue Moon Tavern (women's)

I liked him
I loved him
I loved him
I let him
I let him
I lost him

Costa's (women's)

I try to take life as it comes—
and hope it keeps cummin'

Rainbow Tavern (women's)

Your love gives
me such a thrill
but your love
won't pay my bills
I want
your money
Virginia Inn (women's)

Murphy he just
works & worries & works
Rainbow Tavern (women's)

If they can send a man
to the moon, why can't
they send them all?
Buckaroo Tavern (women's)

Kiss a prince
Get a frog
Buckaroo Tavern (women's)

Women unite!
Make him sleep on
the wet spot tonight!
The Duchess Tavern (women's)

If you make him
sleep in the wet spot
you may have to make
your own wet spot

G-Note Tavern (women's)

The reason the average
American woman would rather
be pretty than smart is
because the average
American male can see
better than he can think

The Duchess Tavern (women's)

I'd love to drink like a lady
one or two at the most
but one & I'm under the table
and two, I'm under the host

Blue Moon Tavern (women's)

War is male menstrual envy

Roanoke Park Place (women's)

Being on the rag
is a drag

Bogey's on Broadway (women's)

Women don't nag—
men procrastinate
G-Note Tavern (women's)

Women always have to wait
Outside wall, Ethnic Theater

Break the Chains!
Unleash the fury of women as
a mighty force for revolution!
Tunnel from UofW to University Bridge

Eastlake Zoo (men's)

Stop making women
responsible for
birth control
O'Banion's Tavern (women's)

Shaving your legs
is self-mutilation

. . . and then

Only if you're uncoordinated

Comet Tavern (women's)

Women are not:
  Girls, ladies (Amy Vanderbilt's
  male pleasing morons), sluts,
  bitches, gals, guys, chicks,
  broads, etc. We are women.
  Grant yourselves, and all of
  us, this dignity.

. . . and then

Amen! If we lose our sense of
humor we lose our flexibility.
Without that, survival, not
to mention success, will be beyond us.—A woman, a girl, a
person, I am still me.

. . . and then

Give me a break, will ya!

Matzoh Mama's (women's)

Women have many faults
Men have only two
everything they say and
everything they do

The Duchess Tavern (women's)

Here's to the men
    what say they love us
Here's to the men
    we say we love—
Fuck 'um—
Here's to us

. . . and then

Yeah—
    One minute they say they
    love us—then if something
    goes wrong then they hate
    our guts. Men are all
    alike. Fuck 'um.

. . . and then

Ladies
    Sorry, I can't agree. It
    doesn't make for great
    graffiti, but mine's as
    close to perfect as humans
    come, man or woman.

. . . and then

LUCKY YOU
    Buckaroo Tavern (women's)

Please love
the one you're with
    Buckaroo Tavern (women's)

A man is like a bathtub
after you use it—
it's not so hot
Eastlake Zoo (women's)

Champion pussy eater
Time _____
Date _____
Tel No. _____
Eat til you come over & over
... and then

For serious consideration,
please leave resume and
references at the bar. We
Blue Moon women are choosy
Blue Moon Tavern (women's)

Don't throw no toothpicks
in the toilet.
Crabs can pole vault.
... and then

Ah, but can they broad jump?
G-Note Tavern (women's)

Roses are red
Violets are blue
I have the crabs
now so do you
Shakey's West Seattle (women's)

Alex is a stud
Alex is married
Swannie's (women's)

Go for a cucumber!
Roanoke Park Place (women's)

My mother never told me:
If you want it done right
do it yourself

Swannie's (women's)

MEN ON WOMEN & SEX & THINGS

No need to be long-winded here.

Men are horndogs and they can no sooner control their insatiable lusts than they could bluff Jesus with a pair of fours and a three dollar raise.

That so many women so frequently suppress urges that are so similar in the male mind is a constant source of resentment. Frustration results and sometimes causes a man, in moments of despair and drunkenness or just plain horniness, to write intemperate things about women on bathroom walls.

Love:

If you lick my ass
I'll lick your ass

No, she said

I'll lick your ass
first, I said

No

Why not?

You'll tell

No I won't

Yes you will
You'll get drunk
and tell, she said

No I won't
I promise

You will
I know you
You will
            —Bukowski

Comet Tavern (men's)

Give me pussy
or give me death!

Owl Cafe & Goodtime Bar (men's)

Fuck me . . .
Beat me . . .
make me
write bad checks
Virginia Inn (men's)

Right on, right in, right out
Odegaard Library UofW (men's)

My Girlfriend
Says Im not a good
lover. How con
anyone Form an
opinion In 20 Seconds?
Comet Tavern (men's)

Sex instructions
for engineers:
1. In
2. Out
3. Repeat if necessary
Physics Building UofW (men's)

Women of the world!
Rise from the beds
of your oppressors . . .
and go make breakfast
Suzzallo Library UofW (men's)

Ah yes,
the old in & out
Peter's Inn (men's)

Why did God invent women?
Because sheep can't cook
Suzzallo Library UofW (men's)

The best friend of
the one-eyed trouser
snake is the bearded
clam.
HUB UofW (men's)

A boy for pleasure
A woman for duty
but a melon for ecstasy
—old Arab saying
University Pizza (men's)

Two, four
six, eight
Are you sure
You're really straight?
Rainbow Tavern (men's)

I would rather
stick my hand
in a baseball glove
than in anything else
Daily newsroom UofW

Foot Fetishists
Fellowship on Friday
(meets at Nordstrom's)
Roswell's (men's)

I like 'em best when
they sit on my face
. . . and then
Why? Is your nose
longer than your dick?
Charlie's Tavern (men's)

Bonermania is for real
Roswell's (men's)

To blow me
is to know me
Swannie's (men's)

Getting head is a
deeply religious experience
Suzzallo Library UofW (men's)

She regarded with exuberance
my cylindrical protuberance
Cause Celebre (unisex)

I'd rather be screwing
Greenhouse Tavern (men's)

Gentlemen:
  Beware of Herpes
Owl Cafe & Goodtime Bar (men's)

Herpes is better
than no love at all
Sundance (men's)

A pussy in the mouth
is worth a cold sore
on the tongue
Roanoke Park Place (men's)

BETTER LAID THAN NEVER
Comm Building UofW (men's)

If women are made
of sugar and spice
how come mine
smells like tuna fish?
Buckaroo Tavern (men's)

How can you tell when
a VAA has an orgasm?
She drops her nail file.
Red Onion Tavern (men's)

Where are the foxy
women in West Seattle?
   1. Alki Beach
   2. I'm desperate,
      where's the dogs?
   3. Call PAWS
Jigsaw Caberet (men's)

Bodin sez:
   Up with skirts!
   Down with pants!
   Physics Hall UofW (men's)

Physics Building UofW (men's)

I get more pussy than you
and being married don't count
Goldies on the Ave (men's)

Where's the best place
to pick up women? (Seriously)
　　1. The morgue
　　2. Savery Hall
　　3. The ankles
Suzzallo Library UofW (men's)

Women:
　　Discount rates for great sex
　　now available. (Includes a
　　really enjoyable discourse
　　with charming male-type).
CALL BEFORE MIDNIGHT
TONIGHT!
**Art Building basement
locker area UofW**

Support women's sports
Run around with a fast lady
Sundance Tavern (men's)

With a nickel
for every good woman
you meet every day—
you could walk
down to Safeway
and buy yourself
a Milky Way candy bar
with spare pennies
left over
for the muscular
dystrophy jar
Greenhouse Tavern (men's)

Asked the blonde waitress
if she'd like to fuck. She
said, "Only if you got 12
inches." I said, "I ain't
gonna bend it in half for
nobody."

G-Note Tavern (men's)

Mine's Bigger

Comet Tavern (pool room)

I wish my dick wouldn't touch
the cold water when I shit

. . . and then

Put the seat down, dumbshit

Suzzallo Library UofW (men's)

If your dong is too short
or your pump too weak
stand a little closer
or you'll piss on your feet

Soundtrack Tavern (men's)

I've Lost two
women in one year
what's wrong with me?

Virginia Inn (men's)

Masturbation is
the poor man's fuck

Buckaroo Tavern (men's)

I'm so horny
even the crack
of dawn ain't safe

Comet Tavern (men's)

Oh John lets not park here
Oh John lets not park
Oh John lets not
Oh John lets
Oh John
Oohhhh

Virginia Inn (men's)

She offered only
puppy love when only
doggy love would do

Eastlake Zoo (men's)

HALF-ASSED PHILOSOPHY AND MERE BULLSHIT

Have you every wondered about the meaning of life?

This next chapter explains that. The thing about graffiti is, it's written by normal people like me and maybe you instead of writers and philosophers and oddballs like that who think too much. God, I hope you're not one of those!

If not, you should obtain from this chapter a remarkably unsophisticated, but extremely pragmatic world view. You'll come out ahead in this world and you'll have me and whoever I stole this graffiti from to thank.

Consider this unsolicited testimony from my chauffeur:

> Dear Boss,
>
> I red your book & liked it. The half-ass philosophy and more bullshit section was best because it was just like you talkin and me listining. Thanks for making me reed it.
>
> Harlan Smatz

And thank you, Harlan. Turn, please.

Close the screen
door but let the
smile show through
Comet Tavern (women's)

I want to love life
but life just
wants to be friends
Daily newsroom UofW

Where its At
Is Always changing
Eastlake Zoo (men's)

When I was a fighter pilot
for the FBI, I discovered
God as the hard-boiled egg
in my lunch box. I ate him.
Blue Moon Tavern (men's)

There are some nights
when the moon howls
and the wolves are silent
Found all over

Fly in the
face of all odds
Comet Tavern (women's)

Mass is best
. . . and then
High mass is better
. . . and then
Nah, weight is better
. . . and then
Give me volume!
. . . and then
Give me speed
. . . and then
Give me enough speed
to overcome volume

Elliott Bay Cafe (men's)

Angels can fly
'cause they take
themselves lightly

Ravenna Co-op (unisex)

I'd rather have a
bottle in front of me
than a frontal lobotomy

The Duchess Tavern (women's)

Cocaine is God's
way of letting you
know that you are
making too much money

The Duchess (women's)

He who dies with
the most toys, wins!
Roanoke Park Place (men's)

Money is NOT
the report
card of life
Central Tavern (men's)

I'd rather have
dope and no money
than money & no dope
. . . and then
I'd rather have money
and no dope than be a
dope with no money
Murphy's Pub (men's)

All progress is based
upon a universal innate
desire of every organism
to live beyond its income
—Samuel Butler
Blue Moon Tavern (women's)

When I die bury me in a
deep place, two speakers at
my feet, some headphones
on my head
and play
The Grateful Dead
Roanoke Park Place (men's)

Our heroes die in hotels
Tunnel from UofW to University Bridge

Bill the Cat
Live like him
Buckaroo Tavern (men's)

Don't urp out
sleep . . . sideways
Comet Tavern (men's)

You can waste a moment
of your life
but don't waste your life
in a moment
Watertown (women's)

Do not Turn
Over 10,000 RPMs

Goldie's on the Ave. (men's)

Live each day like
it was your last!
One day you're going
to be right, dickbreath!
Goldie's on the Ave. (men's)

SPAWN & DIE
Allegro (men's)

Eat, shit, & die
Blue Moon (men's)

Work, Buy, Consume, Die
HUB UofW (men's)

Live, think, do, choose
Art Building UofW (women's)

Let's have some
fun for a change
Art Building UofW (women's)

Stop counting
and start Living
Tunnel from UofW to University Bridge

Give me a steak, a
full tank of gas and
a life of living off
the interest of my money
G-Note Tavern (women's)

Give me:
    A stout ship
    a running sea
    and a wind
    that follows fast
Comet Tavern (men's)

Just think . . .
Somewhere there
is sunshine and a
nice beach to lie on
Comet Tavern (women's)

I have absolutely nothing
against work. I could
watch it all day long
    —W.C. Fields
Comet Tavern (men's)

Do it tomorrow
Kincaid Hall UofW (men's)

Once is not enough for anything
Comet Tavern (women's)

Sex is PEOPLE
Odegaard Library UofW (men's)

Love is the answer still
Liberty Tavern (men's)

Love is NOT a fading violet
but a tenacious weed
that flourishes in the dark

Comet Tavern (men's)

John Lennon talked all
about love, but he couldn't
love his own father. It's
easy to love humanity (It
doesn't exist). It's hard to
love people, people who
aren't perfect. Oh Yeah!
Dig it! Sing it again . . .
Gowen Hall UofW (men's)

Let this
be a lesson
don't be messin'
with love
Blue Moon Tavern (men's)

Some say—
    Two heads are
    better than one
I wonder if being
two-faced applies as well
    Comet Tavern (pool room)

Before you live
you have to give
    The Duchess Tavern (women's)

Give and you shall receive
... and then
Depends on what you give, eh?
    Allegro (unisex)

Give me head
'til I'm dead
    Comet Tavern (men's)

The only absolutes are:
    —the large devour the small
    —cannibus
    —shake it three times
    and you're playing with it
Roanoke Park Place (men's)

Work is the curse
of the drinking class
SeaFarer Tavern (men's)

GOD
   BLESS
       GUINNESS!
Murphy's Pub (men's)

I drink—therefore I am
Odegaard Library UofW (men's)

I'm pink
therefore I am
Grand Illusion (women's)

I stink
therefore I am
       —Desfartes
Virginia Inn (men's)

To do is to be
　　—Socrates
To be is to do
　　—Plato
Dobe Dobe doo
　　—Sinatra
Found all over

Get over yourself
Comet Tavern (women's)

The most confused
minds are often the
most thoroughly convinced
of their own pre-eminence
. . . and then
The most pre-eminent
minds are often the
most thoroughly convinced
of their own confusion
. . . and then
Most confusion doesn't
mind its own pre-eminence
. . . and then
I am pre-eminently
confused by the above
. . . and then
I'm confused as hell!
. . . and then
And I, merely pre-eminent
Blue Moon Tavern (men's)

It doesn't
take a genius
to take a good shit

Comet Tavern (men's)

He who shits on the road
finds flies on his return

Roanoke Park Place (men's)

Eat shit
2,000,000,000,000,000,000
flies can't be wrong

SeaFarer Tavern (men's)

Eat brains

Wall at Pike Place Market

Eat enough dead
animals and finally you
become a dead animal

Roswell's (men's)

Don't count
your chickens
before they're dead

Jazz Alley (men's)

He who
hesitates
is lunch!
—Charles Darwin

Roanoke Park Place (men's)

Skating away
on the thin ice
of a new day

Blue Moon Tavern (men's)

My karma ran over my dogma
. . . and then
Who was driving, your mama?

Ravenna Co-op (unisex)

When faced
with adversity
Go for the glamour!

Comet Tavern (women's)

I'm not in this world for
a goddamned fashion show!
. . . and then
I am and I get $125.00 an hour

Comet Tavern (pool room)

You can fall on your face
bending over backwards, too
Rio Cafe (women's)

Only by attempting
the impossible can one
achieve the ridiculous
Last Exit (unisex)

You can do anything!
Comet Tavern (women's)

Be a joke unto yourself
—Rajneesh
Roswell's (men's)

Old women
fast wine
loose cars
Rainbow Tavern (men's)

What is madness
but nobility of spirit
at odds with circumstance?
—Ted Roethke (Courtesy
of your secretary)
Blue Moon Tavern (women's)

Reality is useful
it occupies the
time between fantasies
Last Exit (unisex)

Reality is the
shifting face of need
Savery Hall UofW (men's)

There is less than ideal
circumstances in this
fallen world that calls for
a corresponding adjustment in
action aimed at fullfilling
universal obligations
Roswell's (men's)

Life is not necessarily
something that I would
recommend to everybody
Rainbow Tavern (women's)

Strive to be happy anyhow
Jazz Alley (men's)

Keep the faith—
there is
no rainbows
without the rain
G-Note Tavern (women's)

The sun shines
People forget

Physics Hall UofW (men's)

*May the best of this year
be the worst of next year*

Matzoh Mama's (women's)

Life is good
You are life

Vacant Building 2016 1st Ave

Friendliness
Compassion
Happiness
　—The triad philosophy of
　　Burger King, McDonalds,
　　Jack-in-the Box

Roswell's (men's)

You can't
buy friendship
but you can sell it

Sundance Tavern (men's)

You can pick your friends
You can pick your nose
but you can't
pick your friend's nose

The Duchess Tavern (women's)

Mucus makes life bearable
Comet Tavern (pool room)

Every silver lining's
got a touch of gray
Comet Tavern (women's)

Jesus lives in me
but he won't pay the rent
Suzzallo Library UofW (men's)

Jesus saves
Buddha invests
Costa's (women's)

TRUST IN GOD—
BUT TIE YOUR CAMEL FIRST!

Comet Tavern (women's)

God is dead . . .
but don't worry
Mary's pregnant again
Red Onion Tavern (men's)

What will save the world?
(our collective asses)
1. sex
2. drugs
3. rock
4. roll
5. Ian Drury
6. less work/more eros

Rainbow Tavern (men's)

Trust in Jesus

Found all over

The reason men make war is:
It's the only thing they can
do that women won't laugh at
... and then
Ha! Ha!
Love Betty

Comet Tavern (men's)

Under the University Bridge
is a piece of graffiti—
"Stupid humans." It seems
simply an echo of an earlier
sentiment—"Lord, what fools
these mortals be!"

Physics Hall UofW (men's)

Let he who cannot
be taught to fly higher
be taught to fall faster

Rainbow Tavern (men's)

**Vacant Penney's Bldg,
Second & Pike**

If the floor fits, wear it

Rio Cafe (women's)

The race is over
the rats have won

Roswell's (men's)

The average working person
is not stupid, just tired
—Studs Terkel
Watertown (women's)

The meek shall
inherit the earth
they are too weak to refuse
Comet Tavern (men's)

The worst taskmaster
is a former slave
. . . and then
Look at Israel
. . . and then
Give me an airplane
Blue Moon Tavern (men's)

a pleasure shared
is a pleasure diminished
D.A.F. DeSade

HUB UofW (men's)

When things get weird
the tough beat up the weird
—V.I. Lenin
Comet Tavern (men's)

Ain't a whore
I couldn't worship
or a saint
I couldn't fuck
Roswell's (men's)

Stevie Wonder was born blind
but that's all right
he's still out of sight!
Blue Moon Tavern (women's)

Love is blind
      God is love
Stevie Wonder is blind
Therefore
      Stevie Wonder is God
Blue Moon Tavern (women's)

Just remember
Dog is God spelled backwards
Morningtown (unisex)

We are prisoners of language
Savery Hall UofW (men's)

We are all sad poems
      —TSF
Odegaard Library UofW (men's)

Espresso Yourself
Elliott Bay Cafe (men's)

"When in doubt
tell the truth"
—Mark Twain
"When in doubt
book 'em"
—Steve McGarret, Five-O
HUB UofW (men's)

Did it ever occur to you
that you might be right?
Odegaard Library UW (men's)

Your potential is as big
as you allow it to be
Comet Tavern (women's)

A mind is
like a parachute
it only functions
when it's open
Suzzallo Library UofW (men's)

Obedience is suicide
Comet Tavern (pool room)

When you're up to your ass in
alligators you forget that your
mission was to drain the swamp

Red Onion Tavern (men's)

Life's a bitch and
you don't even get puppies

Last Exit (unisex)

I wish I didn't know now
what I didn't know then

Peter's Inn (men's)

No matter how hard
you try not to get
grafted, you will

Unique Bar & Grill (men's)

Life is for the living
Love is for the giving
Money is for the making
Time is for the taking

. . . and then

Your ass is for the kicking

. . . and then

Yours is for the sticking

Eastlake Zoo (men's)

Life is like a sewer
You get out what you put in
Savery Hall UofW (men's)

Tell me what men think
when they don't have to think
and I'll tell you what they are
Odegaard Library UofW (men's)

Who is Kilgore Trout?
. . . and then
Who isn't
J&M Cafe (men's)

Entrophy sucks
University Bookstore (stairwell)

Man don't live
by dread alone
Last Exit (unisex)

Be rational
Be productive
Be happy with yourself
and do it my way
Grand Illusion (men's)

I've never
met a struggle
I couldn't succumb to
Allegro (men's)

Learn to forget
Learn to forget
Learn to forget
Learn to forget
Virginia Inn (women's)

Learn to be a child again
Odegaard Library UofW (men's)

Let them drink
Cola beverages
until their ears ring
Comet Tavern (men's)

Sometimes
The things that I do
Don't feel as real
as they really are

Blue Moon Tavern (women's)

Atlas is going to shrug

Odegaard Library UofW (men's)

When all is
said and done
a lot more is
said than done.

Buckaroo Tavern (men's)

CORRECT & PROPER SYNONYMS FOR THE MALE ORGAN

Wasn't it embarrassing last Thanksgiving when your Aunt Winnie asked you to reel off ten quick synonyms for the word "penis" and you only knew eight? Next time you'll be ready courtesy of this list inscribed on the bathroom walls of The Last Exit by civic-minded volunteers.

1. dick
2. prick
3. weenie
4. cock
5. bone
6. P.P.
7. Peter
8. dong
9. pud
10. wanger
11. pocket rocket
12. schlong
13. joystick
14. schwanz
15. Jake the
    one-eyed snake
16. little bald mouse
17. gun
18. pistol
19. sex shooter
20. long action
21. twang
22. John Thomas
23. steaming stalk
24. Ralph
25. slow guitar
26. Mickey Finn
27. turkey neck
28. crank
29. wazoo
30. short arm
31. ramrod
32. spitting dolly
33. tallywhacker
34. muscle of love
35. Gooeyduck

36. pubic probe
37. banananana
38. love pump
39. boner
40. throbbing muscle
41. tool
42. knoble knob
43. hard-on
44. phallus
45. chile (Mexican)
46. organ
47. dink
48. knockwurst
49. tubesteak
50. Oafani
51. Mr. Chesterfield
52. appendage
53. hot nozzle
54. 40-40
55. prong
56. unit
57. love club

POLITICS

Politics was made for graffiti like sewage lagoons were made for chunks of scum.

Graffiti is a critical medium and any time you get a bunch of people together and tell them to go ahead and make some rules, the results will be so laughable as to actually beg criticism.

A final comment. You will notice that most of the graffiti in this chapter is of the liberal persuasion. There is a reason for this—Republicans don't write graffiti. Republicans have far too much respect for property to deface it with unsanctioned statements. Oh, maybe if there was some money in it, sure, but certainly not just for fun.

According to the United States Department of Statistics That Don't Matter But Are Costly To Collect, 93.4 percent of all political graffiti is written by democrats, socialists and lefthanders. The other 6.6 percent is written by aliens.

No matter who
is on the throne
there sits but an ass
    Cause Celebre Cafe (unisex)

Oh, Oh,
    Nancy's in charge
Comet Tavern (pool room)

Ronald Reagan
    I know what I like
    and I like what I know
Art Building UofW (women's)

Ronald Reagan
AMERICA'S
favorite placebo

Rainbow Tavern (men's)

Ron Reagan and
George Orwell in '84
    Suzzallo Library UofW (men's)

Why does Ronald Reagan
only take the bottom posi-
tion when in bed with Nancy?
. . . and then
Because he can only fuck up.
    J&M Cafe (men's)

Ronald Reagan
      fascist gun in the West
Buckaroo Tavern (men's)

Feed the hungry,
feed the poor,
Vote for Reagan's
second term
support the next war
    The Duchess Tavern (women's)

**Vacant Penney's Building,
Second & Pike**

Ronald Reagan is to peace
as finger fucking is to panty hose
Comet Tavern (women's)

We are the Pequod
Reagan is Ahab!
Allegro (men's)

I like Ronald Reagan
I like everything about him;
. . . except his sense of humor
Gowen Hall UofW (men's)

A vote for Reagan
is a vote for Nixon
Rainbow Tavern (men's)

The difference between a
Nixon Presidency and a
bucket of shit is the bucket
Odegaard Library UofW (men's)

Re-elect Nixon
'76
'84
. . . and then
Yes, we should never
have changed "Dicks"
in the middle of a screw
Odegaard Library UofW (men's)

Nixon now!
Let's get
back to zero!
. . . and then
For zero try Ike
he got Dickie the job

Roanoke Park Place (men's)

NO NEWS is AGNEW

University Bar & Grill (men's)

Wally and the Beaver in '84
Found all over

Bert Lance
repossesses house
trailers from truckers'
widows with six kids
Comet Tavern (pool room)

John Anderson in '84
Suzzallo Library UofW (men's)

There . . .
was a young Senator from Mass
who wanted a new piece of ass
he lucked out and found her
but fucked up and drowned her
and the White House
slipped out of his grasp
Business Building UofW (men's)

Vote No
on yes
Blue Moon Tavern (men's)

Fuck dacron
Virginia Inn (women's)

Don't Californicate Washington
FoCastle Tavern (men's)

Don't shoot 'til you see
the whites of their alligators
Last Exit (unisex)

Calling all
Generals and Majors . . .
Your World War III
is drawing near
Suzzallo Library UofW (men's)

Making war for peace is
like making love for virginity
Suzzallo Library UofW (men's)

What the fuck
Odegaard Library UofW (men's)

Apoliticism—
the last luxury of Americans
Comet Tavern (women's)

Nuclear War Now!
Rainbow Tavern (men's)

Nuke U.S.S.R.
Liberty Tavern

Nuke the gay whales
Owl Cafe & Goodtime Bar (men's)

Nuke a gay whale for Christ
Last Exit (unisex)

Nuke the unborn
gay El Salvador whales
Roswell's (men's)

NUKE SHITHEADS
HUB UofW (men's)

Mutants for Nukes
Odegaard Library UofW (men's)

Freeze now—or burn later
Owl Cafe & Goodtime Bar (men's)

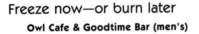

Disarm Now!
... and then
Who's now?
Bloch's on Capitol Hill (men's)

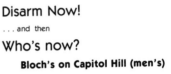

Boeing = Weapons = War
Aurora overpass

Millions for beer
not a penny for defense
Comet Tavern (pool room)

Zuke the Kooks
(belt a kook with
an overcooked zucchini)
Last Exit (unisex)

Capitalism and communism
are not at all alike
in capitalism
it's dog eat dog
while in communism
it's exactly the reverse
McDonald's on Madison (men's)

Marxism Now!
... and then
Is as useless as it was then
Odegaard Library UofW (men's)

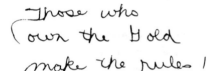

Those who
own the Gold
make the rules!
Goldie's on the Ave (men's)

Fuck the Bourgeois
Virginia Inn (men's)

Eat the rich
Grand Illusion (men's)

Make the rich pay
... and then
10 cents on the dollar
Suzzallo Library UofW (men's)

Hey, Mr. Money, don't kick
me down, cause when the
communists come knocking
they won't be looking for a
handout, they'll come looking
for your head
. . . and then

Like always,
we'll send them yours
Suzzallo Library UofW (men's)

Minimum wages suck!
Lamp Post Tavern (men's)

Make Mick Jagger
pay everybody's taxes
Savery Hall UofW (men's)

The 60's are over
Suzzallo Library UofW (men's)

The hippies
were blithering
pieces of media shit
. . . and then
Too easy, way too easy
Virginia Inn (men's)

YUPPIES GO HOME!
Wall at Bell St. & 1st

Robots on welfare
Suzzallo Library UofW (men's)

*Big Brother isn't coming
yet, but he's breathing hard*

Owl Cafe & Goodtime Bar (men's)

The entire population
is greased and ready
Roanoke Park Place (women's)

WP$$
Suzzallo Library UofW (men's)

Waste gas, it's the American Way
Odegaard Library UofW (men's)

Universities
to propagate
the American Way
Henry's on the Ave (men's)

Did you ever stop to think
that radical ideas that
threaten institutions in turn
become institutions that reject
ideas that threaten institutions?
Education Building UofW (men's)

Get the U.S. out
of the Pacific Northwest!
Last Exit (unisex)

California Red says:
Suzuki
Kawawsaki
Yamaha
Honda
—brought to you by
the people who
gave you Pearl Harbor
SeaFarer Tavern (men's)

Buy a foreign car
put an American out of work
. . . and then

Buy an American car
Reward ineptitude
Savery Hall UofW (men's)

I am red, but I
sure ain't UnAmerican
—Hides-the-Wolf
The Duchess Tavern (men's)

As a fart-creating society,
we no longer have confidence
in ourselves to produce
beyond mediocrity
Allegro (unisex)

Save the whales
collect the whole set
Comet Tavern (men's)

I hate stupid
Bows on underpants
Virginia Inn (women's)

Why is this country so
obsessed with sex choice?
Art Building UofW (women's)

Anita Bryant needs a good fuck
The Duchess Tavern (men's)

Microwave yappy poodles
Virginia Inn (women's)

Smash the State
for fun and Profit
Start with U.S. & Israel
and let's get rid of those
fucking PLO terrorists
while we're at it
College Inn (men's)

Give Utah to the PLO
Savery Hall UofW (men's)

Justice will be done
Reagan will be turned over
to the Salvadoran government
Suzzallo Library UofW (men's)

Conformity is deformity
Grand Illusion (men's)

Dylsexics
Untie!
Roswell's (men's)

If Pro is the opposite
of Con, then CONgress
must be the opposite
of PROgress

**Resource Center North
Seattle Community College (men's)**

Undermine anarchy

Savery Hall UofW (men's)

INDIA
more anarchy than
you'll ever dream

Comet Tavern (women's)

Castrate extremists!

Wall along 50th N.E.

Free the Dave Clark Five!

Murphy's Pub (men's)

Boycott toilet paper!

Odegaard Library UofW (men's)

Frats promote
child-like behavior

Odegaard Library UofW (men's)

Support mental health
...or I'll Kill you
Pete's Place (men's)

Silence those who
oppose free speech
Suzzallo Library UofW (men's)

I hate:
1. poodles
2. Herpes
3. Tuna fish casserole
Virginia Inn (women's)

I HATE E.T.
Comet Tavern (pool room)

The Salvation Army is a cult
Pike Place Market (women's)

Santa Claus must die!
Watertown (men's)

Who killed Bambi?
Rainbow Tavern (men's)

Jimmy Hoffa,
    please call your office
Pete's Place (men's)

Venus di Milo is
alive & well in Argentina
Allegro (unisex)

REAL MEN DON'T EAT
—Bobby Sands
Murphy's Pub (men's)

If Martin Selig did
not exist, would it be
necessary to invent him?
University Pizza (men's)

GOD: Right or wrong
Odegaard Library UofW (men's)

Instead of moaning about
the shitty condition
everything is in—get out
and do something about it
    P.S. No bombs, please
Grand Illusion (men's)

The Jews use the "jive
niggers" to harrass the
working class.

...and then

No—fascists used racism
(and still do evidently)
to destroy the working
class. Politics belongs
on T.V.; not on fairly
respectable bathroom walls

Watertown (men's)

Menachem Begin:
    The first Jewish Nazi

Goldies on the Ave (men's)

Stop supporting
  murderous
Jewish Zionists

...and then

May the Israeli Air Force
bomb your Volkswagon

Grand Illusion (men's)

PEACE, you dum fucker

Goldies on the Ave (men's)

STREET-LIFE GRAFFITI

Living the street life is just as depressing as you would think if street-kid graffiti is any indication. The vacant graffiti found on the vacant Penney's building at 2nd and Pine and throughout the Pike Place Market maze leads to the conclusion that it's a vacant kind of life.

The following graffiti was taken either from walls of the vacant Penney's building at 2nd and Pike or alleyways and night-time gathering spots in the Pike Place Market.

Just too much time

Who knows?

Led for the head

Young upstarts

Mess with the best
Be like the rest

Ya sleep with dogs
and ya get fleas

It's cold out here!

I wish I was thin

Kill cops

Microwave 54 months

Owwwwwww My burning dick

F.B.I. Rats

Stay high 'cause
pigs can't fly

Everybody must get stoned

Hi	Hi	Its	to	you		
Hoe	Hoe	off	work	go		
gonna	a	and	some	Hi Hoe		
get	trick	get	dick	Hi Hoe		
				Hi Hoe		

If you want a good time
call 682 _____. Ask
for Stephan.

Watch your back

kiss ass

give me head now!

Police eat shit!

Conform or be cast out!

Munskin gots a nice body

Get High

Pig fuckers

Steve and Eddie are the
best-looking guys downtown

EPP—a great cheese risk

Voodo on you!

Power isn't all
that money buys

PLO suck Kaddaffi

We are all here
to have some fun
so let it whip

Art Building UofW

You wanted blood
you got it! AC DC

I want to rust
with gay lust

Death to Palestinians!

Anarchy is the way
of the U.S. of A.

Praise the Lord!

Begin, Sharon—War Heroes

Stink Breeze

Tweaky Steve
likes it
in his ass

Jesus Christ is best!

Take a
handful
of qualudes

Why doesn't
Devo
eat potatoes?

Lower heaven

Like it Don't Hide it

Small minds discuss people
Average minds discuss events
Great minds discuss ideas
        —However—
Empty minds
have nothing to discuss

Suzy Creamcheese
eats nasal crackers

U.S. out of El Salvador
& all Salvadorans & every
other foreigner out of U.S.

   Blue Power
Red is just another
color in the rainbow

Turn up the bloody Heat!

!!Beware!!
of needle drugs
coz the only
dope worth
shooting is
Pres. Ronald Wilson Reagan

I was here & you weren't

Mind Power
to be a model
at Pier 70, I wish

Citizen says: Chalk is cheap
      (written in chalk)

JOKES & LIMERICKS

So far we've said mean things about women, men, politics and street punks, but we have a soft spot in our head for these jokes and limericks so we won't say anything.

Roses are red
Violets are blue
I like peanut butter
so let's fuck

Odegaard Library UofW (men's)

Did you hear about the
nymphomaniac with the
receeding hairline?
She's all forehead

Comet Tavern (women's)

My CAR IS CONSTIPATED —
IT CAN'T PASS ANYTHING

Comet Tavern (women's)

There...
was an attorney named Rex
who was sadly deficient in sex
when arraigned for exposure
he replied with composure
"de minimus non curat lex"
(the law is not concerned
with small things)

Blue Moon Tavern (men's)

What do you get when you
cross a gooey duck and an owl?
A mussel that stays up all night.

Buckaroo Tavern (women's)

Sex is like a bridge game
If you don't have a good
partner, you damn well
better have a good hand

The Scarlett Tree (men's)

Why is virginity like a balloon?
One prick and it's gone.

Blue Moon Tavern (women's)

Pregnancy is taking seriously
what was poked at you in fun

Last Exit (unisex)

She offered her honor
he honored her offer
all night long
he was on her and off her

G-Note Tavern (women's)

The God of premature
ejaculation is coming
stay plugged in.

Last Exit (unisex)

Physcists do it
with charged bodies

Physics Hall UofW (men's)

Did you hear about the walrus
that went to a tupperware
party looking for a tight seal?

Elliott Bay Cafe (men's)

Dear Abbey
    I can't remember if my
girlfriend has VD or TB
            signed
            confused

Dear confused
    If she coughs, fuck her

O'Banion's Tavern (men's)

Everybody knows that those
big cats is dangerous but
a little pussy never hurt nobody

O'Banion's Tavern (men's)

How did Herpes
leave the hospital?
On crotches.

Grand Illusion (women's)

Why do dogs lick their genitals?
Because they can.

Virginia Inn (women's)

Carmen so loved her little
Stanislaus, she gave him a bone

Morningtown (unisex)

PAVLOV
Does The name Ring A Bell?

University Pizza (men's)

Life is like a cock . . .
When it's soft you can't
beat it and when it's
hard you get fucked

Buckaroo Tavern (men's)

Did you hear about
the guy with five penises?
Yeah, his pants
fit him like a glove.

Art Building UofW (women's)

What do you get when you
cross a penis with a potato?
A dictator.

Art Building UofW (women's)

Napoleon was here
and beat his Boneapart

Swannie's (men's)

History is a thing of the past
Rio Cafe (men's)

Here I sit broken-hearted
Spent a dime & only farted
Second time I took a chance
Saved a dime but shit my pants
Gowen Hall UofW (men's)

I've shit in London
I've shit in France
but when I came to
Swannies I shit my pants
Swannie's (men's)

Better to fart
and relieve your heart
than not to fart
and bust apart
HUB UofW (men's)

I'm happy here on this toilet
only one thing could spoil it
I'll have to persist
until I have pissed
But . . .
I'm finding it hard to uncoil it
HUB UofW (men's)

If you have consitipation'
tough shit

Odegaard Library UofW (men's)

Start a movement
Eat a prune

Virginia Inn (women's)

I've just solved the
hiddle of tHe Sphincters

Odegaard Library UofW (men's)

Why is toilet paper
like the starship Enterprise?
Because it circles Uranus
in search of Clingons.

Found all over

Those were the days of old
When knights were bold
and toilets not yet invented
They laid their loads
in the middle of the road
and walked away contented

Owl Cafe & Goodtime Bar (men's)

I KNOW I'll NEVER
FIND ANOTHER EWE

Red Onion Tavern (men's)

I am the King of England
I love to sing and dance
and if you don't believe me
I'll kick you in the pants
Watertown (women's)

You can all be nimble
you can all be quick
You can all kneel down
and suck my dick
Odegaard Library UofW (men's)

If Miles Standish had shot
a cat instead of a turkey
we'd all be eating
pussy for Thanksgiving
HUB UofW (men's)

When I'm in a somber mood
I worry, work and think
When I'm in a drunken mood
I gamble, screw and drink
But when my moods are over &
my time has come to pass, I
hope they bury me upsidedown
so the world can kiss my ass
The Duchess Tavern (women's)

Punk sucks
new wave swallows
UofW campus (greenhouse wall)

Some people come here
to shit and stink
others come here
to sit and think
but I come here
to scratch my balls
and read the bullshit
on the walls
HUB UofW (men's)

Some people are all mixed up
their brains are in their bowels
and their heads are full of shit
Swannie's (men's)

There...
once was a girl from Seattle
who loved to go down on cattle
then along came this bull
that unloaded such a fill
it made all her teeth rattle
Peter's Inn (men's)

A STREAKER is ONE who
is unsuited for the OCCASION
Comet Tavern (women's)

Life is like a shit sandwich
The more bread you have
the less shit you eat

Kelley's Tavern (men's)

Cowboys are like flies
they eat shit and bother people

White Pine Tavern (men's)

What's the difference
between an Irish wake
and an Irish wedding?
One less drunk.

Grand Illusion (women's)

Did you hear about
the Irish queer?
He liked girls
better than Guinness.

Murphy's Pub (men's)

Here I sit, cheeks a'flexin
just gave birth to another Texan

Pacific Alaska Forwarders (men's)

What's Irish and sits in the sun?
Paddy O'Furniture.

Swannie's (women's)

We're dwarves
Speak for your elf
Blue Moon Tavern (men's)

What do you get if your cross
a rooster with a telephone pole?
A 30 foot cock who wants to
reach out and touch someone.
Roanoke Park Place (men's)

Hello ladies
The difference between
erotic sex and kinky sex is:
in erotic sex you use a
feather and in kinky sex
you use the whole chicken
The Duchess Tavern (women's)

There...
once was a man from Racine
who built a fucking machine
It had concaves and convexes
that amazed both sexes—
it sure was a bastard to clean
Blue Moon Tavern (men's)

What's the difference between
a sorority chick and a toilet?
A toilet won't follow you
around after you use it.
Roanoke Park Place (women's)

Eight men were shipwrecked
on a small, deserted island:
two Scots, two Irish,
two Welsh and two Englishmen.
After two days the Scots got
together and built a still.
After four days the Irish
had drunk the still dry.
After eight days the
Welsh had formed a choir.
After sixteen days the two
Englishmen were still waiting
to be introduced.

Murphy's Pub (men's)

Round and Round
the earth we go
The moon turns round the earth
the earth turns round the sun
We don't die of old age
We die of vertigo

Bogey's on Eastlake (men's)

I used to think
I was indecisive but
now I'm not so sure

Last Exit (unisex)

Life is like a sorority
one bitch after another after...

The Duchess Tavern (men's)

Roses are red
Violets are blue
Sugar is sweet
and so are you

The roses are wilted
The violets are dead
The sugar bowl's empty
and so is your head
    (famous anti-airhead saying)
Gowen Hall UofW (men's)

There is no gravity
the earth sucks
Found all over

God is perfect
man is not
Man made booze
God made pot
    Last Exit (unisex)

Knock, knock.
Who's there?
Marsupial.
Marsupial who?
Marsupial be comin'
soon as they heat it up.
    Comet Tavern (men's)

What's better than
roses on a piano?
Tulips on an organ.

Roanoke Park Place (women's)

She who stands
on the toilet
is high on pot

Comet Tavern (women's)

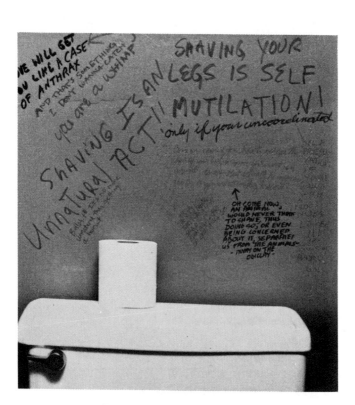

Comet Tavern (women's)

There...
was a young girl from Hoboken
who said her cherry was broken
from riding a bike
on a cobblestone pike
but really, twas broken by pokin
University Pizza (men's)

Tits are like toy trains
they're meant for little
kids but daddy always
gets to play with them
Swannie's (men's)

What's invisible and
smells like a carrot?
A rabbit fart.
G-Note Tavern (women's)

Art is like morality.
You have to draw
the line somewhere.
Costa's (women's)

What do you get when you
cross an ape with a computer?
A Harry Reasoner.
Grand Illusion (women's)

If you don't like
the way I drive
stay off the sidewalk
Grand Illusion (women's)

You can lead a horticulture
but you can't make her think
Found all over

How do you separate the men
from the boys in Seattle?
With a crowbar.
Rainbow Tavern (men's)

Did you hear about
the Polish lesbian?
She likes men.
Comet Tavern (women's)

Old truckers never die
they just get a new Peterbilt
Rainbow Tavern (women's)

Girl: I've lost my virginity.
Boy: Thank God you've still
       got the box it came in!
Buckaroo Tavern (men's)

What are the three hardest years
in the life of a Ballard roofer?
Second grade.

The Scarlett Tree (men's)

What do a nun and
7-Up have in common?
Never had it, never will.

Rainbow Tavern (women's)

Wanna get stoned?
Drink wet cement.

Roswell's (men's)

There was...
a young woman named Alice
who peed in the Vatican Chalice
She said, "I do this
from a great need to piss
and not from Sectarian malice."

Roswell's (men's)

There...
once was a girl from Sydney
who took it up to her kidneys
She met a man from Quebec
who stuck it up to her neck
Sure had a big one, didn't he

Suzzallo Library UofW (men's)

A mathematician named Hall
had a hexagonical ball
the cube of his weight
plus his dick times eight
is his number give him a call
. . . and then

Sorry Hall, not enough info
. . . and then

Hey stupid, all mathematicians
named Hall weigh 170 pounds
and have 4.3 inch dicks

Virginia Inn (men's)

Music Building UofW (sound room)

How do we know
that Jesus was a Jew?
1. He lived at home
   until he was 30.
2. He went into
   his father's business.
3. His mother thought
   he was God.

University Bar & Grill (women's)

Carry me back
to 'Ol' Virginity'

The Duchess Tavern (men's)

MISCELLANEOUS

What can you say about miscellaneous? It's just a bunch of shit that didn't fit anywhere.

Time flies like an arrow
Fruit flies like bananas
Belltown Cafe (women's)

Paul was the walrus. Honest.
—John Lennon
Comet Tavern (pool room)

Hang on D.B.!
We'll be there soon
Blue Moon Tavern (women's)

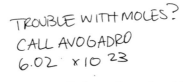

TROUBLE WITH MOLES?
CALL AVOGADRO
6.02×10^{23}

Buckaroo Tavern (men's)

The shit has hit the fan
send lawyers guns & money
Buckaroo Tavern (men's)

Gold fish have a
more interesting sex
life than you think
Pete's Place (men's)

I love my bear!
Physics Hall UofW (men's)

Heterosexual toe-sucking orgy
(Only on Tuesday)
Don't bite off
more than you can chew
Art Building UofW
(basement locker area)

I would not be convicted
by a jury of my peerverts
Grand Illusion (men's)

I'm full of shit
and anal retentive
Rainbow Tavern (men's)

Shit all you like
but hang on to your brains
Kort Haus Tavern (men's)

INTRODUCING
The Official
John Wayne Toilet Paper
It's Rough
It's Tough
And it don't take no
shit off of any asshole!
Greenhouse Tavern (men's)

Due to cutbacks, toilet paper
is now for faculty use ONLY
. . . and then
Students can use
their degrees anyway
Kincaid Hall UofW (men's)

Profanity is the crutch
of the ignorant fuckhead
Merchant's Cafe (men's)

Someday, someone important
will sit here and then you'll
be sorry for what you've written
Last Exit (unisex)

Cat's ass
Rat's ass
Dirty old twat
69 douche bags
tied in a knot
—Tom Waites
Suzzallo Library UofW (men's)

Here, here,
hip hip,
and all the bullish
Last Exit (unisex)

Only 361 days 'til Christmas
Tugs (men's) 01-04-83

Rocky & Bullwinkle!
Sat. at 10:30 Ch. 13
Batman at 11:00
Business Building UofW (men's)

Steve wants money
Wall near Pike Place Market

I want to suck a owner
. . . and then
I want to own a sucker
Virginia Inn (men's)

Swallow Fritz—
An American hero
Merchant's Cafe (men's)

What- if they gave
an orgy & nobody came?

Comm Building UofW (men's)

Beyond narcism
. . . and then
I want to go
Matzoh Mama's (women's)

Finally I bring a pen and
can't think of a thing to write
Watertown (men's)

Here by the sea & sound
nothing ever goes as planned
Watertown (men's)

If you want to look & feel
like a soft-minded teenage
schmuck, get a haircut at
_____. Ask for Dave,
a vicious misogynist.
Art Building UofW (women's)

Maybe you're not paranoid
maybe they're really after you
Roanoke Park Place (men's)

Punks are some
dum-looking pinheads
. . . and then
Written by a jock in a
baseball hat & IZOD shirt
Goldies on the Ave (men's)

Your mama eats
Lima Beans. Do you?
Buckaroo Tavern (men's)

Empty Space
   Support it
   You're one, too!
Comet Tavern (women's)

I may not agree with
your bumper sticker,
but I will defend to the
death your right to stick it
Merchant's Cafe (men's)

Never have so
few written so
little for so many
Grand Illusion (men's)

The '83 prime time
line-up really sucks
Rio Cafe (women's)

Indiana Jones is a pimp
Kincaid Hall UofW (entrance door)

For a good fuck, tell
your girlfriend to call
328 _____ and ask for Paul
Goldies on the Ave (men's)

Dead goats priced to move
Liberal discounts for trade-ins

Bagley Hall UofW (men's)

Silver Ego was here

Last Exit (unisex)

I just gotta MICTURATE!

Physics Hall UofW (men's)

From an Ann Arbor
grad passing through:
Beautiful campus, but where
the hell are your resident
preachers, characters, odd—
balls, social outcasts? They
make college life so much
more interesting.

. . . and then

Did you check
the faculty lounge?

Suzzallo Library UofW (men's)

Woody Sullivan is alive
& well, living on Pluto in a
Revere Ware pressure cooker

Physics Hall UofW (faculty, men's)

BASIC RULE:
I before E
except after C
WEIRD
Swannie's (men's)

Go to school 'til you
puke because you'll puke
immediately upon going to work
University Pizza (men's)

I wanna be sedated
Last Exit (unisex)

John Halfmoon,
the doctor is operating
White Pine (men's)

Heaven is
a place where
nothing ever happens
. . . and then
So is Bellevue, but
I don't want to go
there when I die

Rainier Pub (men's)

Seattle native—
an endangered species
Dantes (men's)

Every 10 seconds a woman
gives birth to a child.
That woman must be
tracked down and stopped.
Suzzallo Library UofW (men's)

If you're not paranoid
you're not paying attention
Roanoke Park Place (men's)

Herpes is the gift
that keeps on giving
Suzzallo Library UofW (men's)

Loose hips sink ships
Scarlett Tree (men's)

TRADE OR SELL
ONE BLIND CRAB
for two with NO teeTH

Pacific Alaska Forwarders (men's)

Vassar College has
only three urinals
on the whole campus
Roswell's (men's)

I can't find my proclivities

... and then

Did you check your anal cavity?

Ravenna Co-op (unisex)

How do you spell relief?

1. Columbian
2. Thai stick
3. Masturbation
4. T.V.
5. Sensimmilian
6. Kona buds
7. Beethoven
8. Cocaine
9. A healthy shit
10. LSD
11. Fly fishing
12. D-E-A-T-H

Odegaard Library UofW (men's)

Comet Tavern (pool room)

Merciful Snatch
©1982
All rights RESERVED

Savery Hall UofW (men's)

Suicide is the most sincere
form of self-criticism

Victoria Station (men's)

All the wisdom of the
universe can be bought
with one book—The Bible
... and then
But if you order BEFORE
midnight tonight, it's yours
for just $9.95—plus you get
the steak knives & organ
peeler as your special gifts
Suzzallo Library UofW (men's)

Jesus Saves
... and then
and Esposito
knocks in the rebound
Owl Cafe & Goodtime Bar (men's)

Who was in Haight-Ashbury
in 1967-69?
1. I don't remember
2. I was in Buffalo, sorry.
3. I was there on a field trip
4. I saw it on T.V.
5. Scott McKenzie
Roanoke Park Place (men's)

Black is beautiful
Tan is grand
But white's the color
of the Big Boss Man
Raintree near Sea-Tac (men's)

People who use the phrase
"totally awesome" should be:
1. Made to breast feed
   Shamu the whale
2. Disemboweled
3. Made to watch every
   single rerun of Love Boat
4. Visited by talkative
   Jehovah's Witnesses
Music Building UofW (sound room)

Don't forget to remember
to forget what you forgot
Roswell's (men's)

Don't be a wise ass
—Plato
Roswell's (men's)

Do not write on the wall!
. . . and then
So you want we should type?
The Attic (men's)

Please don't write on these
walls—that's what the black-
board is for, you asshole.
   —The management
. . . and then
But it lacks permanence
University Bar & Grill (men's)

Only dip shits write
on shit house walls...
oh fuck, what's that make me?
Goldies on the Ave (women's)

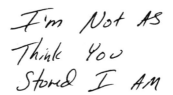

I'm Not As
Think You
Stored I AM

Odegaard Library UofW (men's)

I would never recommend
drugs, alcohol or violence
—BUT—
They've always worked for me
—Hunter S. Thompson
Greenhouse Tavern (men's)

Yes, you
can survive
on drugs alone
Music Building UofW (sound room)

Death before dishonor
Drugs before lunch
Comet Tavern (pool room)

Powder to the People
Daily newsroom UofW

Give me librium
or give me meth
Daily newsroom UofW

Playing defender on
acid is the greatest
Odegaard Library UofW (men's)

Drugs: Use them
. . . and then
Drugs: Die from them!
. . . and then
The only people who
die from drugs are
the ones too stupid to
know a gram from an ounce
Savery Hall UofW (men's)

Drugs saved my life
Irish Pat's Saloon (men's)

Drugs are for people
who can't handle reality
Blue Moon Tavern (men's)

Reality is for people
who can't handle drugs

Owl Cafe & Goodtime Bar (men's)

Acid consumes 47 times
its weight in excess reality

Owl Cafe & Goodtime Bar (men's)

Don't drop acid
Take it pass/fail

Daily newsroom UofW

Whatever happened
to good drugs?

J&M Cafe (men's)

It was fun while it lasted
too bad it lasted longer
than it was fun

Watertown (women's)

Hugs
Not
Drugs

Cause Celebre Cafe (unisex)

It must be beer-thirty again

Buckaroo Tavern (men's)

I had too much
to drink last night

Suzzallo Library UofW (men's)

Comet Tavern (pool room)

I fucked your mother!

... and then

Go home Dad, you're drunk

Found all over

I don't know if I should
shit or wind my watch.
As a matter of fact, I
think I'll shit on my watch.
—Groucho Marx

White Pine Tavern (men's)

Picking your nose
is out of the question

Rainbow Tavern (men's)

I wish I could sleep

O'Banion's Tavern (men's)

She works the day shift
and he works the night

Rainbow Tavern (women's)

Jack off with silk panties

Suzzallo Library UofW (men's)

I never jacked off or
lied in my entire life
—Fulls Hit

Goldies on the Ave (men's)

You can beat it
on the toilet seat
You can slam
it on the wall
But not until you've
zipped your pants
will that last drop fall

**Library North Seattle
Community College (men's)**

Stand Proud!
    You're holding the
    future of America
    in your hands

**Owl Cafe & Goodtime Bar (men's)
located above urinal**

I think men have nice tits

. . . and then

Me, too

. . . and then

Try cows for greater variety

. . . and then

That is udderly ridiculous

. . . and then

Can't top that one

Last Exit (unisex)

I'll never leave Bellevue again
Daily newsroom UofW

Society is arbitrary and
therefore meaningless, if
you so choose. Life is sprung
from selection of random vari—
ants and has no direction or
purpose other than what you
hold to be true. Reject the
values and goals of American
culture. Use your brain to
choose your own. This is not a
return to the caves, for we have
evolved past that. This is
not Social Darwinism, for that
is barbaric.
. . . and then
Whatever happened
to fun graffiti?
Suzzallo Library UofW (men's)

Betty eats Barney's Rubble
Odegaard Library (men's)

People
People who eat
People
are the hungriest
People
Daily newsroom UofW

Doug loves Mary
Doug loves Mary
Doug loves Mary

Dianne loves Doug
Dianne loves Doug
Dianne loves Doug

Mary loves Dianne
Mary loves Dianne
Mary loves Dianne
Art Building UofW (women's)

Better Gay than Grumpy!
Virginia Inn (women's)

Gay is the way
... and then
to rectal problems
Shakey's, West Seattle (women's)

Wanted:
Pregnant lesbian for anal
sex. Use dildo to fuck me
while I am dressed like a
goose. Must be open to
experiments with blenders.
Savery Hall UofW (men's)

Love between two people is
beautiful any way it happens
. . . and then
What could possibly happen?
Art Building UofW (women's)

This is the spot!
Be here everyday
(07/01 to 08/01)
at 4:30 to 5:00 p.m.
. . . and then
FUCK OFF!
. . . and then
I think that's his idea
Physics Hall UofW (men's)

Why don't the gay people take
over a straight bar for a change?
The Broadway (men's)

Minnie Mouse is a dyke
Comet Tavern (women's)

Let's hear it for the
lesbians of Seattle.
There are more than
enough of us to be
heard. We are everywhere.
Bogey's on Broadway (women's)

My father made a lesbian
My mother made a lesbian
... and then
If I give her the material
will she make me one, too?

Comet Tavern (women's)

Susie is a lesbian
but at least
she's not a secretary

Comet Tavern (women's)

I'm gay, but at least part
of me is VERY straight

Music Building UofW (sound room)

Fuck you, Holden Caulfield!

Rainbow Tavern (men's)

Fuck you, Fraternity man!
... and then
I wouldn't enjoy it.
I'd just lay there.

Suzzallo Library UofW (men's)

Brown shoes don't make it

**Resource Center North
Seattle Community College (men's)**

There's a lot of shit
going down around here
. . . and then
Oh?

Odegaard Library UofW (men's)

If you took a shit here, please
give it back. No questions asked.
—The management

Buckaroo Tavern (men's)

You're all fools

Eastlake Zoo (men's)

Fresh Lutefisk—
a contradiction in terms

Blue Moon Tavern (men's)

Helen noticed by now that
the musty smell had returned.
But what to do? John would
be coming home with his new
boss at any moment . . .

Music Building UofW (sound room)

Hmmmmmmmmn?
Fresh air smells funny

Virginia Inn (men's)

I miss you
my beloved
Alaska
Virginia Inn (women's)

Alaska
What America
used to be
Rainbow Tavern (men's)

U.S. out of Ecotopia now!
Odegaard Library UofW (men's)

Drop the BIG ONE and get it over
with. The suspense is killing me.
Roanoke Park Place (men's)

Chapter 1
The last man on earth,
resigning himself, packed
his pipe with the rest of
his buds. There was a knock
at the door . . .
Buckaroo Tavern (men's)

THE GROSCARS

Yes, the paralyzing suspense is nearly over!

Finally, the time has arrived for the awarding of the prestigious Groscars.* The individual graffitos which have managed to stand out above all others in their categories will now be recognized for their outstanding contributions to, uh...whatever.

So that the glamour and excitement of this moment will never be forgotten, the winners will be immortalized by induction to the Wall of Fame, that yellowed bathroom wall that stanktifies everything that is ignoble about the wonderful medium of graffiti.

The Wall of Fame is, as even the least traveled among you surely must already know, located in Smelterville, Idaho in the men's room of Billy's Slag Heap Tavern, just down the alley from Mine Shaft #9b.

Because many of you have been unable to force yourselves to visit this attraction, a representation of the section that will hold this year's winners follows immediately after the awards.

*Pronounced Grawskars

*Best graffito in a
supporting role .... Put the seat down,
dumbshit
(In support of: I wish my
dick wouldn't touch the
cold water when I shit!)

*Best short subject .... We're dwarves
Speak for your elf

*Distinguished Public
Service Award .... Rocky & Bullwinkle! Sat. at
10:30 Channel 13
Batman at 11:00

*Best graffito in an
ironic role............ Castrate extremists!

*Best educational
graffito .... BASIC RULE
I before E
except after C
WEIRD

*Best Advice .... You can fall on your face
leaning over backwards, too

**Best Graffito .... When I was a fighter pilot
for the FBI, I discovered God
as the hard-boiled egg in my
lunch box. I ate him.

I wish
my Dick
wouldn't touch
the COLD WATER
when I shiT

Put THE SEAT DOWN
DUMBSHIT

Basic Rule
I before E
except after C.
Weird

You can fall on your
face bending and
backwards, too

When I was a fighter pilot
for the FBI, I discovered
God as the hard-boiled egg
in my lunch box. I ate him.

CASTRATE
EXTREMISTS

ROCKY & BULLWINKLE
SAT AT 10:30 CHANNEL 13
BATMAN @ 11:00

We're Dwarves
Speak
for your
elf